Pretty BOOKMARKS

BY DEBORAH LAMBEIN

Leisure Arts Inc. • Maumelle Arkansas

X	DMC	ANC.	COLOR	X	DMC	ANC.	COLOR
	210	108	lavender		776	24	pink
	563	208	green		841	378	brown
	744	301	yellow		3755	140	blue

Bookmark #5
Bookmark #6
Bookmark #7
Bookmark #8

GENERAL INSTRUCTIONS
WORKING WITH CHARTS

How to Read Charts: Each of the designs is shown in chart form. Each colored Square on the charts represents one Cross Stitch.

The Chart are accompanied by a color key. This key indicates the color of floss to use for each stitch on the charts. The headings on the color key are for Cross Stitch (**X**), DMC color number (**DMC**), Anchor color number (**ANC.**), and color name (**COLOR**). Color key columns should be read vertically and horizontally to determine type of stitch and floss color.

Where to Start: The horizontal and vertical centers of each charted design are shown by arrows. You may start at any point on the charted design, but be sure the design will be centered on the bookmark. Locate the center of the bookmark by folding it in half, top to bottom and again left to right. On the charted design, count the number of squares (stitches) from the center of the chart to where you wish to start. Then from the bookmark's center, find your starting point by counting out the same number of fabric threads (stitches).

STITCHING TIPS

Preparing Floss: To ensure smoother stitches, separate strands and realign them before threading needle. Keep stitching tension consistent. Begin and end floss by running under several stitches on back; never tie knots.

STITCHDIAGRAMS

Counted Cross Stitch (X): Work one Cross Stitch to correspond to each colored square on the chart. For horizontal rows, work stitches in two journeys *(Fig. 1)*. for vertical rows, complete each stitch as shown *(Fig. 2)*.

Fig. 1
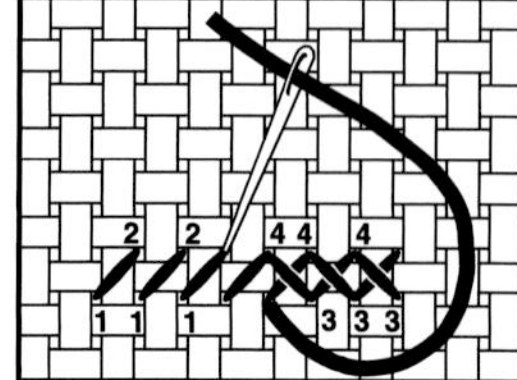

Fig. 2
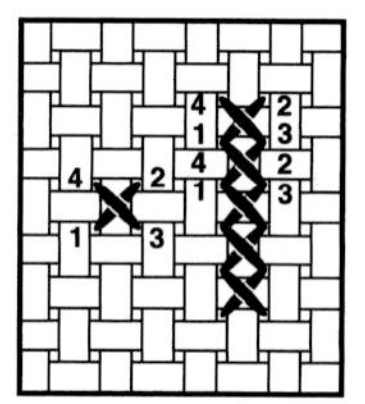

PROJECTS

Note: Cover models were stitched on White Stitch-n-Mark™ Bookmarks (18 ct) using 2 strands of floss for Cross Stitch.

Bookmark #1 — approx design size 1³/₈" x 6"

Bookmark #2 — approx design size 1³/₈" x 6"

Bookmark #3 — approx design size 1³/₈" x 6"

Bookmark #4 — approx design size 1³/₈" x 5⁷/₈"

Bookmark #5 — approx design size 1³/₈" x 6"

Bookmark #6 — approx design size 1³/₈" x 6"

Bookmark #7 — approx design size 1³/₈" x 5⁷/₈"

Bookmark #8 — approx design size 1¹/₄" x 5⁷/₈"